A Note to Parents

Dorling Kindersley *Readers* is a
for beginning readers, designed
leading literacy experts, includi
President of the National Read
board member of the International Reading Association.

D0361183

   Beautiful illustrations and superb full-color
photographs combine with engaging, easy-to-read
stories to offer a fresh approach to each subject in the
series. Each Dorling Kindersley *Reader* is guaranteed
to capture a child's interest while developing his or her
reading skills, general knowledge, and love of reading.

   The four levels of Dorling Kindersley *Readers* are
aimed at different reading abilities, enabling you to
choose the books that are exactly right for
your child:

Level 1 for **Preschool to Grade 1**
Level 2 for **Grades 1 to 3**
Level 3 for **Grades 2 and 3**
Level 4 for **Grades 2 to 4**

   The "normal" age at which a child
begins to read can be anywhere from
three to eight years old, so
these levels are intended only as a general
guideline.

   No matter which level you select,
you can be sure that you are helping
your child learn to read, then read to
learn!

LONDON, NEW YORK, SYDNEY, DELHI, PARIS,
MUNICH and JOHANNESBURG

Publisher Andrew Berkhut
Editor Regina Kahney
Art Director Tina Vaughan

Reading Consultant
Linda Gambrell, Ph.D.

Produced by the NFL Publishing Group
Editorial Director John Wiebusch
Managing Editor John Fawaz
Art Director Bill Madrid

First American Edition, 2001

2 4 6 8 10 9 7 5 3 1
Published in the United States by DK Publishing, Inc.
95 Madison Avenue, New York, New York 10016

ISBN: 0-7894-7880-3 (PB)
ISBN: 0-7894-7879-X (HC)

A Catalog Record is available from the Library of Congress.

Color reproduction by Hong Kong Scanner.
Printed in China.

Photography credits:
t=top, b=below, l=left, r=right, c=center,
All photos (except *) copyright NFL Photos
and these photographers
Courtesy AAU: 23*; Courtesy Boys Town: 45; Mary Ann Carter:
36; Chris Covatta: cover br, 35; Greg Crisp: 40; David
Drapkin/NFLP: 27; Hand & Hammer: 25*; Michael C. Hebert:
11; Paul Jasienski: 31; Allen Kee: 3, 19, 39; Courtesy Olivia
Manning: 13; Al Messerschmidt: cover c, 21; Steven Murphy: 4;
NFL Photos: 9; Al Pereira: 7; Mitchell Reibel: 47; Joe Robbins:
41, 44, 46; Bob Rosato: 24; Brian Spurlock: 15, 29, 49; Paul
Spinelli/NFLP: 6; Jamie Squire/Allsport: 17; Kevin Terrell/NFLP:
18; The Topps Company: 22; Ron Vesely: 2, 32, 42, 48.

see our complete
catalog at
www.dk.com

Contents

READING
3
ALONE

PEYTON
MANNING

Written by James Buckley, Jr.

DK

Born to play

The strong quarterback with the youthful face and the powerful arm barks out the signals to his team.

"Blue 42! Blue 42! Hut, hut!"

The center snaps the ball to the quarterback's hands, and players suddenly jump into action. Bodies slam into each other, and wide receivers race downfield.

The quarterback drops back, cool and calm amid the action. He spots his receiver running past the defense...one, two, three, *zing*...he fires the ball down the field like a rocket.

Almost faster than you can believe, the ball is in the receiver's hands. One giant step later, the receiver is in the end zone, and the crowd roars.

The young quarterback dashes to the end zone to congratulate his teammate. It's another touchdown pass for Peyton Manning and the Indianapolis Colts!

Peyton Manning is one of the NFL's top young stars.

Peyton Manning is one of the NFL's best young players. In only three seasons in the NFL, he has set records, led his team to the playoffs, and been selected to the Pro Bowl.

Manning didn't come from obscurity to star in the NFL. From the time he was a little kid, he has been aiming for the top. With hard work, natural talent, and the support of family and friends, he has made his NFL dream come true.

It's only natural that pro football was his dream. Because Peyton is not the first person in the Manning family to

Pro Bowl
The NFL's annual all-star game is held each February in Hawaii. It is a great honor to be chosen to play in the Pro Bowl.

play the game. Peyton's father, Archie, played in the NFL for 13 seasons.

This is Peyton's story, about how he made his football dreams come true.

Archie and Peyton Manning, a football family

Early days

Peyton Williams Manning was born March 24, 1976, in New Orleans, Louisiana. The Mannings were a football family.

Archie Manning was a quarterback for the hometown New Orleans Saints. Peyton and his brothers Eli and Cooper were big football fans, of course, and sometimes they went to practices with their dad, who later played for the Houston Oilers and Minnesota Vikings.

Peyton played a lot of sports. In fact, he was all-state as a baseball shortstop. But he loved football the most. He and his brothers often played catch; Cooper was a great receiver and was Peyton's favorite target. Eli was a quarterback like his brother and his dad.

Before he joined the NFL, Archie had been a superstar quarterback for the University of Mississippi, which is known as "Ole Miss."

In junior high school, Peyton would stay up at night listening to tapes of his dad's games at Ole Miss.

Archie Manning became a star when he played college football for Ole Miss.

Archie was a big influence on his sons, though he never pushed them into football. But Archie was there to help when needed.

"My dad was very supportive of us," Peyton says. "I have a love for football today because it was fun for me as a kid. I've always had a true love for sports, and I think that's because of the way my dad taught us as kids."

"I encouraged my boys to just play for fun," Archie says. "We played a lot in the backyard. I wasn't trying to make them athletes, I just wanted them to have the experience of playing.

"We had all the neighborhood kids playing together. I still see some of them today, grown up, and they remember how much fun we had."

Peyton (left) and his dad, Archie, at an Ole Miss game.

Peyton learned his lessons well. At Isidore Newman High School in New Orleans, he passed for more than 7,200 yards and led his team to a 34-5 record in four seasons. He had an amazing 39 touchdown passes as a senior and was named the national high school player of the year by two organizations.

One of Archie's key targets was his brother Cooper, a star wide receiver. All that backyard practice paid off when brother caught a touchdown pass from brother.

By this time, Archie was working as a radio announcer for the New Orleans Saints. He took Peyton to a team practice, and the young quarterback got a chance to throw to NFL players for the first time.

Peyton was national high school player of the year.

Because Archie went to Ole Miss for college, everyone expected Peyton to go there, too. Peyton received hundreds of letters begging him to attend Mississippi. It was a difficult decision because many other colleges also wanted him to play football and study at their schools.

But Peyton knew that Archie would trust him to make the right decision and would support him no matter what he decided.

Finally, after carefully going over his options, Peyton chose the University of Tennessee. Ole Miss fans were sad, but Peyton stuck to his decision.

"For every person who was disappointed that I chose Tennessee, there were ten people supporting my decision to go there," Peyton says.

"My father supported me. And that's all that mattered."

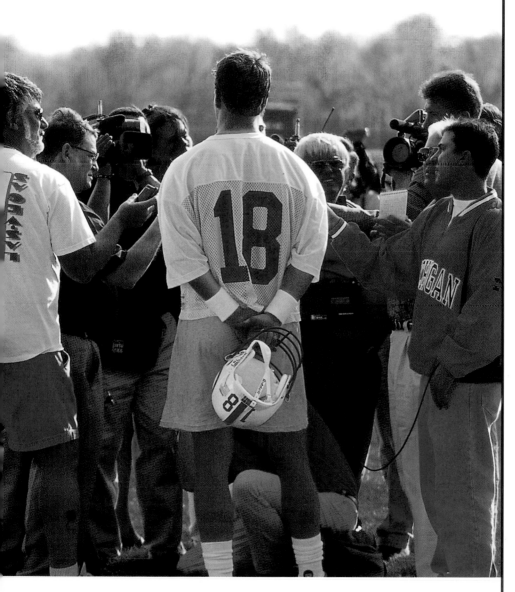

Everyone has a question for Peyton to answer.

He's a Volunteer

Although Ole Miss fans were disappointed, Tennessee fans were overjoyed. The entire state was excited to have this great young passer on the team, which is known as the Volunteers or "Vols."

In the bright orange uniform of Tennessee, Peyton quickly proved he belonged in the college game.

He expected to back up the first- and second-string quarterbacks, but they were injured early in his freshman season. Suddenly, the kid from New Orleans was the starter.

Peyton came through in a big way. He was named the freshman of the year in the Southeastern Conference (SEC). He helped his team win the Gator Bowl.

At Tennessee, Archie (right) continued to support Peyton.

Why Volunteers?

University of Tennessee sports teams are called Volunteers because the state motto is "The Volunteer State."

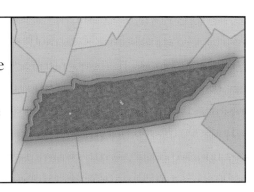

He made mistakes, of course. Young players do that. But experts saw that Peyton had special gifts.

Peyton had all of the physical skills to succeed: a great arm, quick feet, and terrific vision. But it was his knowledge of the game that made him special.

Peyton continued his success as a sophomore, which is what a second-year college student is called. He set several school records and helped the Volunteers win the Florida Citrus Bowl.

In 1995, Peyton threw 380 passes, and only 4 were intercepted (caught

In the pocket
Blockers form a circle around a quarterback while he tries to pass. The place the quarterback stands is called the pocket.

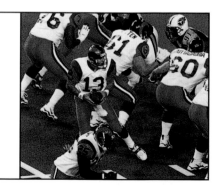

by the opposing team's defense). That set a collegiate record for interception percentage, which measures how often a quarterback's passes are intercepted.

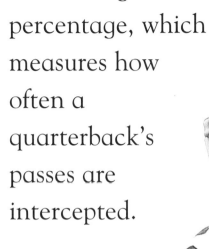

Manning in action at Tennessee

In 1996, as a junior, Peyton had another great season. He set the school record for passing yards, and Tennessee won the Florida Citrus Bowl again.

After doing so well as a junior, Peyton considered leaving school to join the NFL. Some very talented players choose to cut their college careers short and turn pro.

Peyton would surely have been a high draft choice in the NFL, and he had already earned his college degree in speech communications. Many people expected him to leave Tennessee.

But he decided to stay.

"I didn't want to look back and say I wish I would have stayed," Peyton says today. "So I decided to stay all four years.

"I had my degree, so I had a chance to create a lot of memories for myself. I just wanted to enjoy being a senior."

Peyton took the Vols to new heights.

He did more than enjoy his senior season—he loved it! In 1997, Peyton led Tennessee to one of its greatest seasons. The Vols won the SEC title and were ranked as high as third in the nation.

In a victory over Kentucky, he passed for 523 yards and 5 touchdowns, his best performance in a college game.

Peyton became the winningest quarterback in SEC history, with 39 victories in four years. He held almost every Tennessee passing record.

He was second in the voting for the Heisman

Johnny U.
Johnny Unitas was one of the NFL's greatest quarterbacks. He played for the Colts from 1956-1972.

Trophy, which is awarded annually to the top college player. He won the Johnny Unitas Golden Arm award for being the top quarterback, and the Sullivan Award, given to the top U.S. amateur athlete in any sport.

Peyton shows off his Sullivan Award.

Peyton also earned awards for his schoolwork. He was a three-time Academic All-America. He was named Phi Beta Kappa [Fie BAY-ta KAP-pa], a special award for top students.

Phillip Fulmer was Peyton's coach at Tennessee.

In Peyton's final college game, the Vols lost to a powerful Nebraska team in the Orange Bowl, but Peyton was glad he had stayed in school.

The school and its fans loved Peyton so much they changed the name of the street outside the university's Neyland Stadium to Peyton Manning Pass.

"Peyton raised everybody's play around him," said Tennessee coach Phillip Fulmer. "That was because of his competitive spirit, ability, and leadership. He was a difference maker."

Next stop: the NFL.

Key to Success
Top students receive this special silver "key" for being named Phi Beta Kappa. The letters on the key are Greek.

Welcome to the pros

With his years at Tennessee over, Peyton could look ahead to the NFL, the ultimate dream of every player.

The Indianapolis Colts and the San Diego Chargers had the top two picks in the 1998 NFL draft.

Peyton surely would be chosen by one of those two teams—but which one? There was another great young passer named Ryan Leaf, from Washington State, who some people thought might be better than Peyton.

The Colts had the first pick.

"With the first pick of the 1998 NFL draft," read NFL Commissioner Paul Tagliabue [TAG-lee-uh-boo], "the Indianapolis Colts select Peyton Manning, quarterback, Tennessee."

Peyton's NFL dream had come true. Now it was up to him to make it all he wanted it to be.

NFL Commissioner Paul Tagliabue congratulates Peyton at the NFL draft.

In 1998, football became a full-time job for Peyton Manning. In college, he spent time going to class, being with friends, and enjoying Tennessee.

In Indianapolis, Peyton spent almost all of his time focused on football. Even though he was a great player, he still had a lot to learn about being a quarterback and a leader.

"I was expected to be the team leader while learning how to be a pro," Peyton remembers. "That was a major challenge. The club had taken a risk drafting me. They had banked their future on one player...me!"

But Peyton was up to the challenge. Just as he had at Tennessee, he had a terrific first season. Peyton the rookie became Peyton the star.

Success in the NFL comes from practice, practice, practice.

Peyton was named the Colts' starting quarterback before the season began. He showed that Indianapolis had made the right choice when he started every game and didn't miss an offensive play the entire season.

Peyton set NFL rookie records for touchdown passes, passing yards, attempts, and completions.

But Peyton still was learning. Along with his 26 touchdown passes, he threw 28 interceptions. That was quite a change for a player who once threw only 4 interceptions in a season.

The Colts were a young team and struggled against the top clubs. Even with Manning setting many rookie records, the Colts finished with a 3-13 record, one of the poorest in the NFL.

Peyton felt the heat as an NFL rookie.

"I lost more games my first season in the NFL than I did during my entire high school and college careers," Peyton says. "I knew I was going to lose some in the pros, but I couldn't let that drag me down. I had to learn from every mistake I made."

Peyton also learned about life away from college and home. Along with learning about football, he learned about being a star athlete.

He knew that his celebrity could help other people, and Peyton worked with several community groups that assisted disadvantaged children.

Meanwhile, the work on the field continued. Peyton and his teammates knew they could get better. In 1999, the Colts got a lot better.

Triple threat

Peyton knew that one of the most important "teams" in football is the quarterback and the top wide receiver. On the Colts, that receiver was the speedy Marvin Harrison.

After the 1998 season, Peyton and Marvin spent most of their days together, working hard to become better.

They memorized each pass pattern in the Colts' playbook, working on a single play each day until they knew it.

While Peyton and Marvin worked to get better, the Colts added new players to help the team improve. One of the most important was rookie running back Edgerrin [EDGE-er-in] James, who was a great receiver, too.

Peyton loads up to throw a pass.

Pass patterns

Receivers go out for passes by running routes they decide before the play. These routes are called pass patterns.

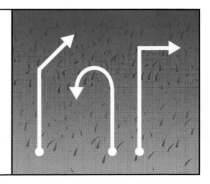

"The big difference for me from 1998 to 1999 was that, as a rookie, I hoped that I would complete a pass," Peyton says. "In 1999, with a year under my belt, I *knew* I would complete the pass."

Marvin Harrison (88) and Edgerrin James helped the Colts succe

Peyton's confidence was a key ingredient to the Colts' amazing 1999 season. After winning only three games in 1998, they won 13 in 1999. That 10-game improvement in their record is the best in NFL history.

Peyton had an outstanding season, setting a Colts' record with 4,135 passing yards. He extended a streak he had begun in 1998 to 27 games in which he completed a touchdown pass.

Marvin Harrison led the NFL with 1,663 receiving yards, while Edgerrin James led with 1,553 rushing yards, the fourth-highest total ever by a rookie.

It was only the second time in NFL history that a team had a trio with 4,000 passing yards, 1,500 receiving yards, and 1,500 rushing yards.

The triple-threat offense made the Colts one of the most exciting young teams in the NFL.

The teamwork between Peyton and Marvin was crucial in an important game against Miami. With the score tied 34-34 and time running out, Peyton hit Marvin with two long completions. The plays set up a game-winning field goal as time ran out.

After beginning the season 2-2, the Colts won an incredible 11 games in a row. They won the AFC Eastern Division title. But the Colts' season ended with a disappointing loss in the playoffs.

Peyton knew there was room to improve. Before the 2000 season, he and his teammates began their hard work all over again.

Peyton and Marvin Harrison made sure they knew the Colts' offensive plays in and out. This time, however, they were joined by Edgerrin James.

Peyton thinks the closeness he has built with his teammates helps when they take the field.

"If you're going to get in the huddle with guys when the game is on the line in the fourth quarter," Peyton says, "it's nice to be leaning on guys that you like. That is a big part of our team's success."

Before the 2000 season, many people expected the Colts to play in the Super Bowl because of their great record the year before. To get their run for the title started, the Colts actually left the country.

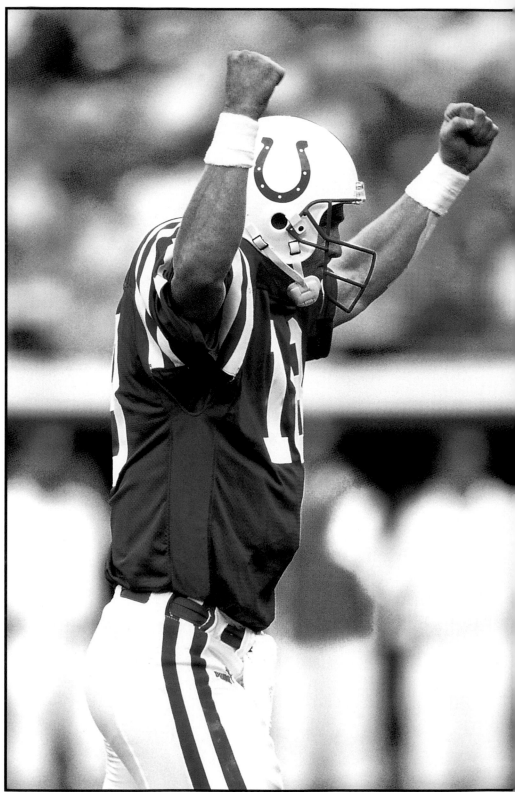

The Colts played a preseason game in Mexico City, just as Archie Manning had done with the Saints in 1978.

"I've always enjoyed doing some of the things my father did in the NFL," Peyton said. "That we both played in Mexico was very special."

One thing that Peyton did that his father didn't was play on winning teams. Archie played for 13 years but usually on teams that weren't very good. He never made the playoffs, while Peyton made it in his second season. Peyton has been lucky to be part of a great team.

In 2000, the trio of Manning, James, and Harrison continued to work well together. Though they lost in the first round of the playoffs, Manning and the Colts are ready for success in the future.

It's PeyBack time

While Peyton Manning and the Colts continue to shoot for a Super Bowl, Peyton continues his work off the field helping people.

"I think athletes are role models who should show kids about respect, responsibility, and persistence in

 achieving goals," Peyton says.

He formed the PeyBack Foundation to help kids in Indianapolis, New Orleans, and other places. The

foundation sponsors many programs, including the PeyBack Classic, a high school all-star football game played in Indianapolis each summer that raises money for college scholarships.

Peyton also worked with a foster children's group, helping to coach at a flag football clinic. Imagine catching a pass from Peyton Manning.

Also, working with a hospital in Indianapolis, he created Peyton's Playbook, a workbook that shows kids healthy habits for life.

In addition, Peyton joined the NCAA Foundation, an organization that helps college student-athletes.

On the field or off, whether he's passing to his teammates or to some kids in the park, Peyton Manning is a true winner. He was born to play...and born

to care about others.

"I'm one of the lucky people who grew up in a home where nothing was more important than my family," he says. "I'd like to help other kids enjoy that same love."

Career statistics

Here are Peyton Manning's statistics for his first three NFL seasons. You can fill in future seasons in the spaces provided.

Year	Att.	Comp.	Pass yds	TDs
1998	575	326	3,739	26
1999	533	331	4,135	26
2000	571	357	4,413	33
2001	___	___	___	___
2002	___	___	___	___

Glossary

Amateur [AM-uh-chur]
In sports, athletes who are not paid to play, such as college students, are called amateurs.

Attempts
Passing statistic that counts how many times a quarterback throws a pass.

Completions
Passing statistic that counts how many of a quarterback's passes are caught by a teammate.

Draft
The annual selection of college players by NFL teams; held each April in New York City.

End zone
The 10-yard-deep areas at each end of the football field. Carrying or catching the ball in the end zone scores a touchdown for your team.

Huddle
Before most plays, each team gathers together, often in a circle, to plan the next play; this circle is called the huddle.

Interception
A pass that is caught by the defense instead of the offense.

Pass patterns
Receivers run along preplanned paths on the field on each play; these paths are called pass patterns or pass routes.

Playbook
NFL teams have a large set of plays and play diagrams for offense, defense, and special teams. Each player receives a playbook that contains all these plays. Some teams use a CD-ROM instead of a binder or book.

Playoffs
Games played after the regular season to determine the league champion.

Pocket
A roughly circular area formed by blockers to protect the quarterback.

Pro Bowl
The NFL's annual all-star game, played between teams from the AFC and NFC each February in Hawaii.

Sack
Defensive play in which the quarterback is tackled behind the line of scrimmage.

Scholarship
An award of college fees to top athletes or students.

Signals
Before each play, the quarterback yells out signals to his team that help tell it what play the team will run and when the ball will be snapped.

Statistics
Using a wide variety of numbers, averages, and measurements, statistics track the on-field activity of each player and team.